# A SHORT HISTORY
## OF
### EXISTENTIALISM

# A SHORT HISTORY
## OF
# EXISTENTIALISM

BY JEAN WAHL

Translated from the French
by Forrest Williams and Stanley Maron

GREENWOOD PRESS, PUBLISHERS
WESTPORT, CONNECTICUT

# CONTENTS

ONE DAY NOT LONG AGO, AS I WAS LEAVING A CAFÉ in Paris, I passed a group of students, one of whom stepped up to me and said: *"Sûrement, Monsieur est existentialiste!"*

I denied that I was an existentialist. Why? I had not stopped to consider, but doubtless I felt that terms suffixed by *ist* usually conceal vague generalities.

The subject of existentialism, or philosophy of existence, has begun to receive as much attention in New York as in Paris. Sartre has written an article for *Vogue*; a friend informs me that *Mademoiselle*, a magazine for teen-age young ladies, has featured an article on existentialist literature; and Marvin Farber has written in his periodical that Heidegger constitutes an international menace. The philosophy of existence has become, not only a European problem, but a world problem.

It is no less of a problem to define this philosophy satisfactorily. The word "existence," in the philosophic connotation which it has today, was first used by Kierkegaard. But may we call Kierkegaard an existentialist, or even a philosopher of existence? He had no desire to be a philosopher, and least of all, a philosopher with a fixed doctrine. In our own times, Heidegger has opposed what he terms "existentialism," and Jaspers has asserted that "existentialism" is the death of the philosophy of existence! So that it seems only right to restrict our application of the term "existentialism" to those who willingly accept it, to those whom we might call The Philosophical School of Paris, i.e., Sartre, Simone de Beauvoir, Merleau-Ponty. But we still have not found a definition of the terms.

We face another difficulty in the paradox that the manner in which most of us speak of the philosophy of existence partakes of what Heidegger calls "the domain of the inauthentic." We SPEAK of the philosophy of existence; this is precisely what Heidegger, and Sartre as well, would like to avoid since we are concerned with questions which, strictly speaking, belong to solitary meditation and cannot be subjects of discourse. And yet we are gathered here today to discuss these questions . . .°

To begin with, we must contrast the philosophy of existence to the classical conceptions of philosophy to be found in, say, Plato, Spinoza, and Hegel. For Plato, philosophy was the search for Essence, because Essence is immutable. Spinoza sought access to an eternal life which is beatitude. Gener-

° The substance of the text was originally delivered in a lecture in 1946 in France at a meeting of the *Club Maintenant.* The slightly revised form translated here was prepared by the author himself.—Tr.

ally speaking, the philosopher has wished to rise above the realm of Becoming and find a truth universal and eternal. He has generally operated—or so he believed—solely by reasoning. One might say that the last philosopher of this kind was Hegel, who carried farthest this effort to understand the world rationally. On the other hand, Hegel differed from the others by his insistence upon Becoming and the importance which he assigned to this notion. Already, in this sense, he had diverged from the tradition of Plato, Descartes, Spinoza, and many others. Nevertheless, Hegel believed in a universal reason. He tells us that our thoughts and feelings have meaning solely because each thought, each feeling, is bound to our personality, which itself has meaning only because it takes place in a history and a state, at a specific epoch in the evolution of the universal Idea. To understand anything that happens in our inner life we must go to the totality which is our self, thence to the larger totality which is the human species, and finally to the totality which is the absolute Idea. This is the conception which Kierkegaard, whom we may call the founder of the philosophy of existence, came forward to contradict.

Opposing the pursuit of objectivity and the passion for totality which he found in Hegel, Kierkegaard proposed the notion that truth lies in subjectivity; that true existence is achieved by intensity of feeling. To consider him merely as a part of a whole would be to negate him. "One might say," he wrote, "that I am the moment of individuality, but I refuse to be a paragraph in a system." To the objective thinker he opposes the subjective thinker, or, rather, what he calls the individual, the unique. By dint of knowledge, Kierkegaard says, we have forgotten what it is to exist. His principal enemy was the expositor of a system, i.e., the professor.

The existent individual, as Kierkegaard defines him, is first of all he who is in an infinite relationship with himself and has an infinite interest in himself and his destiny. Secondly, the existent individual always feels himself to be in Becoming, with a task before him; and, applying this idea to Christianity, Kierkegaard says: one is not a Christian— one becomes a Christian. It is a matter of sustained effort. Thirdly, the existent individual is impassioned, impassioned with a passionate thought; he is inspired; he is a kind of incarnation of the infinite in the finite. This passion which animates the existent (and this brings us to the fourth characteristic) is what Kierkegaard calls "the passion of freedom."

The notions of choice and decision have an importance of the first order in the philosophy of Kierkegaard. Each decision is a risk, for the existent feels

4

himself surrounded by and filled with uncertainty; nevertheless, he decides. Note that what we have just said concerning the existent's mode of thinking and being discloses the object of his thought: the infinite; for with such infinite passion one can only desire the infinite. Thus, the *how* of the quest gives the goal; and, since we are in contact with this infinite, our decisions will always be decisions between the All and the Nothing, like those of Ibsen's Brand. Under the influence of these passions and decisions, the existent will ceaselessly strive to simplify himself, to return to original and authentic experience.

But so far we have dwelt only on the subjectivistic aspect of Kierkegaard's philosophy. For him, as for the other philosophers whom we will consider, there is no subjective without a certain *rapport* with a being. "The existence of a Christian is contact with Being," he wrote in 1854 in his Journal. The existent must always feel himself in the presence of God and reintegrate into Christian thought this notion of being in front of God. But to feel oneself before God is to feel oneself a sinner. Thus, it is by sin, and particularly by consciousness of sin, that one enters the religious life. But once in the religious sphere, one has still to progress, by a sort of spiritual voyage, from a religion which stays close to philosophy to the highest stage of religion. In the highest stage of religion, reason is scandalized, for we meet with the affirmation of the incarnation in the idea of the birth of the eternal being at a certain place and a certain moment in history.

The existent individual, then, will be he who has this intensity of feeling because he is in contact with something outside of himself. He will undergo a kind of crucifixion of the understanding. He will be essentially anxious, and infinitely interested in respect to his existence because an eternity of pains or an eternity of joys depend upon his relation with God. Thus, he will be in relation with what Kierke-gaard calls "the absolute Other": a God Who, though protective, is absolutely heterogeneous to the individual; an infinite love which, no doubt, embraces us, but which we feel to be other than ourself because in our fundamental individuality and sin-fulness we are opposed to it.

We have noted two ways by which Kierkegaard opposed Hegel: by the emphasis laid upon sub-jectivity, and by the importance assigned to inten-sity of individual feeling. We must add to these distinctions Kierkegaard's insistence upon the idea of Possibility. For Hegel, the world is the necessary unfolding of the eternal Idea, and freedom is neces-sity understood. For Kierkegaard, on the contrary, there are real possibilities, and any philosophy which denies them is oppressive, suffocating. Moreover, the idea of Possibility is linked to the idea of Time, and we may contrast Kierkegaardian time, with all its ruptures and discontinuities, to the logical unwinding of Hegelian time, just as the subjective and passionate dialectic of Kierkegaard has been contrasted to the Hegelian dialectic.

Naturally, the ideas of Kierkegaard pose many problems. On the one hand, is there not a tendency in Kierkegaard to rationalize and explain the paradox by presenting it as the union of the finite and the infinite? And although he purports to present us with a scandal to reason, does he not thereby diminish to some extent the element of scandal? On the other hand, Kierkegaard himself realized that the coming of Christ into the world did not constitute the supreme paradox, which would have been reached only if no one had perceived the coming of God. "I meditate on this question," wrote Kierkegaard, "and my spirit loses its way." Let us add that the paradox exists only for him who dwells below; for the blessed, that is to say, for those who see the truth, the paradox vanishes. In short, this entire construction exists only from an "earthbound" point of view. But perhaps this does not constitute a genuine objection. In a general way it is very difficult to determine whether such observations are objections or whether, by accentuating the paradox, they reinforce the Kierkegaardian conception. We could say the same in regard to questions brought out by the relations between Subjectivity and History (the intensity of the subjective feeling being paradoxically founded upon an objective historical fact), and by the relations between Eternity and History (for, if the moment of incarnation is an eternal moment, the paradox threatens to vanish).

Without a doubt we could trace the history of the philosophy of existence back to Schelling, a philosopher whom Kierkegaard knew, and to the battle waged by Schelling, near the end of his life, against Hegel. To Hegelianism Schelling opposed what he called his "positive philosophy" or his "affirmation of incomprehensible contingency." We may even find in the writings of the young Hegel certain features which are not dissimilar to Kierkegaardian thought; but we must be wary of attributing too much historical importance to the youthful Hegel. Moreover, even the quasi-Kierkegaardian elements which did infiltrate into Hegel's philosophy lost in transit their character of subjective protestation.

We could even trace the philosophy of existence back to Kant, who demonstrated that we cannot conclude existence from essence and thus opposed the ontological proof. Existence ceased to be perfection, and became position. In this sense, we may say that Kant begins a new period in philosophy. Or we may go back to Pascal and Saint Augustine, who replaced pure speculation with a kind of thinking closer to the person, the individual. It remains no less true, however, that we are able to recognize and understand these early prefigurations of the philosophy of existence only because a Kierkegaard existed.

*

*　　*

The second major event in the history of the philosophy of existence occurred when two German philosophers, Jaspers and Heidegger, translated the reflections of Kierkegaard into more intellectual terms.

We may consider the philosophy of Jaspers as a sort of secularization and generalization of the philosophy of Kierkegaard. In the philosophy of Jaspers we are no longer referred to Jesus, but rather, to a background of our existence of which we may glimpse only scattered regions. Humanity has multiple activities, and each of us has multiple possibilities. But we develop one, we sacrifice another, and we never attain to that Absolute which Hegel prided himself on being able to reach through the unwinding of the Idea to its necessary conclusion. The absolute, in Jaspers' philosophy, is "something hidden," revealing itself in fugitive fragments, in scattered flashes like intermittent strokes of lightning. We have the sensation of a night into which our thought or non-thought plunges. Consequently, we are doomed to "shipwreck," *naufrage*; our thought fails utterly, yet fulfills itself in this very disaster by sensing the background of Being from which everything springs.

We know that this background is something real; we derive our reality from it; yet we cannot construe it, and as existents we cannot even express ourselves completely. But in this awareness of defeat, which comes most vividly to us in situations in which we are strained to the utmost, we fully realize ourselves. Whether it be in human drama or in scientific discovery, we sense that there is something other than ourselves, something which exceeds us; and we assert ourselves in our existence by our relation with this transcendence. In this respect, we find in Kierkegaard and Jaspers the same connections between existence and transcendence. To this transcendence, no longer called Jesus (save in some recent writings), Jaspers has given the name *Umgreifend* or "All-enveloping," the other-than-us which encompasses us.

Jaspers senses deeply those values which escape language, science, and objectivity; and the antithesis resident in our experience of transcendence. He also endeavors to complement the Kierkegaardian and Nietzschean intuitions with the profound feeling of human communication and human historicity. For him, we are not isolated, as Kierkegaard would have us isolated. Communication, a struggling love with other persons, is at the core of his system.

Communication has consistently been one of the major problems in the philosophies of existence. Indirect in Kierkegaard, direct and striving in Jaspers, divided into "authentic" and "inauthentic" in Heidegger (the authentic sphere being reserved, it seems, for poetic expression), clumsy and failing in Sartre, communication is always there—at least as a problem. Even in the absence of communication, the idea obstinately persists.

Now let us turn to Heidegger. His problem is the ancient problem of Being. He has declared that he is not a philosopher of existence, but a philosopher of Being, and that his eventual aim is ontological. Heidegger considers the problem of existence solely to introduce us to ontology, because the only form of Being with which we are truly in contact (according to Heidegger) is the being of man. To be sure, there are other forms of Being for Heidegger: there is what he calls "the being of things seen," or scenes; there is the being of tools and instruments; there is the being of mathematical forms; there is the being of animals; but only man truly exists. Animals live, mathematical things subsist, implements remain at our disposal, and scenes manifest themselves; but none of these things exists.

11

In order that we ourselves may truly exist, rather than remain in the sphere of things-seen and things-used, we must quit the inauthentic sphere of existence. Ordinarily, due to our own laziness and the pressure of society, we remain in an everyday world, where we are not really in contact with ourselves. This everyday world is the domain of what Heidegger calls "the anyone" *—or what we might call "the domain of Everyman"—where we are interchangeable with each other. In this domain of "anyone," we are not conscious of our own existence. And an awareness of ourselves as existents is attainable only by traversing certain experiences, like that of anguish, which put us in the presence of the background of Nothingness from which Being erupts.

Kierkegaard insisted upon the experience of anguish, which he compared to dizziness, as a revelation of the possibilities which lie beyond. The Heideggerian anguish, however, does not lead to "mere possibilities," which are partial and relative non-entities, but to Nothingness itself. Through anguish we sense this Nothingness, from which erupts everything that is, and into which everything threatens at every instant to crumble and collapse. This attempt to give reality to an absolute Nothingness (even were we to consider it mistaken) is one of Heidegger's most interesting ventures.

° In German, *das Man.*—Tr.

Naturally, this Nothingness is difficult to characterize. We cannot even say that it *is*, and Heidegger has invented a word, *Nichten* ("naughten"), to characterize its action. Nothingness "naughtens" itself and everything else. It is an active Nothingness which causes the world which erupts from it to tremble to the foundations. One might say that it is the negative foundation of Being, from which Being detaches itself by a sort of rupture. Let us remark parenthetically that in a postscript to the tract in which Heidegger discloses his theory of Nothingness, he tells us that this Nothingness, differing from each and every particular thing which *is*, can be none other, at bottom, than Being itself—for, he argues, what is there different from each thing that *is*, if not Being? Thus, we reach by a different route the identification which Hegel had effected between Being and Non-Being. And this might suggest many problems, e.g., how can one say that it is solely through anguish that Being reveals itself, and that it is into Being that everything may collapse?

In any case, the experience of anguish reveals us to ourselves as out in the world, forlorn, without recourse or refuge. Why we are flung into the world, we do not know. This brings us to one of the fundamental assertions of the philosophy of existence: we are, without our finding any reason for our being; hence, we are existence without essence.

Obviously, we have abandoned any classical scheme, any hierarchy of realities at the top of which is God, the most perfect Being. Now we see only existents, flung for no reason upon the earth, and essences are merely constructions from existences. No doubt one may seek out essences of material things and implements, but there can be no essence of an existent individual, of man. Here we see most clearly the essence—if we may so speak!— of the philosophy of existence, as contrasted to nearly all classical philosophy, from Plato to Hegel, in which existence always derives from essence.

The existence of man, this being, flung into the world, is essentially finite. Limited by death, his existence is a "being for death," as the Kierkegaardian anguish was a "sickness unto death." Although our existence is characterized by the fact that there are things possible to us, the moment will come when there will be no more possibilities, when there will be no more "ahead of us." This is, of course, the moment of death, which Heidegger characterizes as the impossibility of all possibility. It is this fact of our being in a finite and limited time which accounts for the tragic character of Anxiety.

Nevertheless, in this limited world we do accomplish a movement—or rather, movements—of transcendence; not towards God, because God does not exist (this is the principal teaching which Heidegger retains from Nietzsche), but towards the world, towards the future, and towards other people. Thus, the idea of transcendence loses its religious character and acquires, paradoxically enough, a sort of immanent character; it is a transcendence in immanence. Let us note immediately, in reply to any possible objections from those who might insist that transcendence implies in common philosophical parlance a religious affirmation, that Heidegger observes the word "transcendence" ought to denote the end towards which we are going; properly speaking, to transcend is to rise towards. Thus, a being such as God could never be a transcendent being. Only man can transcend.

Let us examine more closely these various transcendences. First, there is transcendence (or, for those who still shy away from this term: "passing beyond") towards the world. We are in-the-world, so to speak. We are naturally outside of ourselves: this is the signification, according to Heidegger, of the word "existence," which suggests an egress. By way of signifying the same idea, Heidegger says that existence is naturally *ecstatic*, in the primitive meaning of this term. Curiously enough, few philosophers have insisted upon our essential participation or relationship with the world. At the outset of his Meditations, Descartes cast doubt upon the reality of the world. Kant questioned his idea of the world. Whereas, for Heidegger, we are always "open to the world." In a brilliant passage in one of his lectures, Heidegger compared his theory to Leibniz's monadology. The monads, said Leibniz, have neither doors nor windows, each monad being entirely self-enclosed. According to Heidegger, individuals are likewise doorless and windowless, but this is true not because individuals are isolated, but because they are *outside*, in direct relation with the world— in the street, so to speak. Individuals are not "at home," because there are no homes for them.

Second, not only are we always and as a matter of course in natural relation with the world, but we are in immediate relation with other existents. And here, this theory which first presented itself as an individualism becomes an affirmation of our natural, even our metaphysical, relation with other individuals. Even in our most individual and private consciousness, even when we think we are most alone, we are not separated from others. "Without others," says Heidegger, is another mode of "with others."

Third, we go beyond ourselves towards the future. Each of us is always in front of himself. We are always planning, and we project ourselves into the plan. Man is a being who is constantly oriented towards his possibilities; the existent is a being who *has* to exist. In this connection, we may say that the time of existence begins with the future. In fact, what Heidegger calls *das Verständnis*, or Comprehension, is always stretched towards the future. And thus it is that we are always filled with anxiety or care. We are always concerned with something which is yet to come; and Being, in so far as we seize it in existence, is care and temporality.

It is clear that these three transcending movements are not quite analogous to transcendence as conceived by Kierkegaard and Jaspers, since they are transcendences within the world and paradoxically immanent to it. We surpass ourselves, but always in the circle of the intramundane.

We have been at pains to examine three movements of transcendence which enter into Heidegger's philosophy. Two more transcendences complete the list: transcendence of the existent from Nothingness ("on the substratum of Nothingness"), and transcendence from "particular things which are" towards Being (a transcendence to which we have already alluded). In summary, transcendence towards the world, towards other men, towards the future, towards Being, and transcendence out of Nothingness are the five uses of the idea of transcendence to be found in Heidegger. We may feel that in this multiplicity of meanings there are sources of ambiguity.

We have noticed that we are always ahead of ourself. On the other hand, like the One of the second
hypothesis of Parmenides,° we are always "younger"
than ourself. Moreover, because we are flung into
the world, we find ourself with such-and-such a de-
terminateness and such-and-such a constitution, in
such-and-such a place and time. This means that we
are not only our future; we are also our past. One
might say that we have to find ourself—the expression "we have to" implying futurity, and the
expression "ourself" implying both futurity and
pastness. We have also noticed that our future is
limited by the fact that at the terminus there is
always death as the impossibility of possibility. Our
future is again limited by the fact that our possibilities are not abstract ones, but rather, are em-
bedded in specific conditions not chosen by the
individual.

Thus, we move ceaselessly from our future to our
past, from our anticipations and plans to our mem-
ories, regrets, and remorses. This fact of being constantly in touch with both the future and the past
constitutes a third term in the vocabulary of Heidegger: the third ecstasy of Time. Being both before
and behind ourself, we are in the same Time as ourself. Consequently, for Heidegger the third ecstasy
of Time, or the Present, is in some sense the product

° *Plato*, Parmenides (Steph. 152).—Tr.

of the juncture of our future and our past. We may fix upon this idea as the starting point of Heideggerian ethics, from which he conceives an act of "Resolute Decision" by which we take upon ourself our past, our future, and our present, and affirm our destiny. Here, for the second time we may note, in passing, the possibility of comparing the philosophy of Heidegger with the philosophy of Nietzsche. We may also compare it, as always, with the philosophy of Kierkegaard. We may perceive the influence of Kierkegaard on Heidegger's theory of "Everyman"; on the notions of anguish, suffering, and sin; on the pre-eminence accorded to Future (a pre-eminence, to be sure, which also appears in the philosophy of Hegel); and even on the notion of a "resolute decision."

It is important for a proper understanding of Heidegger that we do not consider these notions as a series of philosophical dogmas. According to Heidegger, man, unlike other beings, interrogates himself. In fact, man *is* that being who questions, endangers, and puts at stake his very existence. We noted that the philosophy of existence is essentially the affirmation that existence has no essence (thereby going further than merely stating that essence comes after existence). But we may add, as a second characteristic of the philosophy of existence, that one's existence, because it is without essence, is the risk itself. Inasmuch as man is in-the-world, and is the being who is a philosopher in his own being, man endangers, when he questions himself, the world which he is developing, in some sense, around himself.

If we take the first Heideggerian definition of philosophy to be the endangering of Being by a being, the second definition, derived by Heidegger from his own etymological interpretation of the word "philosophy," is "the wisdom of love" (not, as usually derived, "the love of wisdom"). If we understand by wisdom the communion of ourselves with things, philosophy becomes the acknowledgement of our selves as beings-in-the-world. Philosophy becomes knowledge of the existent, not only in so far as he is oriented towards his future, as Kierkegaard defined him, but also in so far as he is in ecstatic relation with the world. From this point of view, the philosophy of Heidegger is an expansion, and in a certain sense, a negation of Kierkegaardian individualism. We must recognize the injustice of reproaching this philosophy for immuring us in ourself; on the contrary, it declares that there is no subject-object dichotomy and that the classical conception of the Subject must be exploded to reveal us as always outside of ourself—this latter phrase, indeed, ceasing to have any meaning, since there is no "ourself" to be outside of.

In putting himself in danger, man endangers the whole universe which is bound to him. In every philosophical question, the totality of the world is implicated at the same time as the existence of the individual is self-endangered and cast into a supreme gamble. Thus, we see the ideas of individuality and totality, and we may even add, the ideas of individuality and generality, constantly reuniting. In fact, Heidegger speaks not merely for one particular individual; he speaks for every individual. He is describing human existence in general. Anguish is doubtless a particular experience, but through Anguish we arrive at the general conditions of existence, or what Heidegger calls "the Existentials." In this respect the philosophy of Heidegger claims a further distinction from the philosophy of Kierkegaard, in that Kierkegaard always remains in the existential, whereas Heidegger attains Existentials, that is to say, the general characteristics of human existence. One may well ask if the notion of essence is not reinstated in the philosophy of Heidegger, and if Kierkegaard is not more consistent in his banishment of this notion. One may ask further if the search for Existentials and for Being is compatible with affirmations of existence.

Perhaps the most important question of all concerns the kind of ethical conclusions which may be drawn from these conceptions of Heidegger. Simply stated, we may say that, finding ourselves forlorn and abandoned in the world, we must shoulder our human condition and—as has already been intimated—assert our destiny. The existent is not to remain in the stage of anguish; or the stage of nausea, as it is described by Levinas and Sartre, two philosophers of existence whose reflections are linked in origin to the ideas of Heidegger. According to each of these philosophers, man can and must triumph over this experience. Man may take upon himself his own destiny, by what Heidegger calls "the Resolute Decision," which is comparable to "Repetition" in Kierkegaard and to the active consent to eternal recurrence which culminates the philosophy of Nietzsche.

Heidegger has not completed his philosophy. *Being and Time (Sein und Zeit)* is the name of his great work, and, in fact, one sees that for Heidegger the very nature of Being is constituted of temporality, and that he strives to bring Space itself into one of his moments of Time, i.e., the Present: thereby assenting, to a certain extent, to the Bergsonian theory of Space and Time. Nevertheless, one cannot say that his ontology is complete. One may even raise the question of why it is incomplete, and whether there may not be an irreducible duality between existence and the search for Being. The only way to Being is through existence. Can one found an ontology upon this existence? Such, it seems, is the Heideggerian problem.

Since the publication of *Being and Time*, Heidegger has attempted, in certain tracts, to erect a kind of philosophy more myth-like than mystic, in which he enjoins us to a communion with the earth and the world, invoking to this end the thought of Holderlin and Rilke. On the other hand, he has made a painstaking study of the idea of Truth; but there too, it seems, he is confronted with antinomies and wavers between a fundamental realism and an idealism of freedom not unlike that of Fichte.

Recalling his distinction between different forms of being, one may well ask if the being of the implement, and even the being of the scene, does not imply the human being. This question brings to the foreground the whole problem of idealism in Heidegger. No doubt, he would like to pass beyond the antinomy of idealism-realism. Nevertheless, it seems (save in certain passages of particular profundity) that he is forced to be now a realist, now an idealist, and that he does not succeed in passing beyond the domain in which these two doctrines stand in opposition, despite all his desire to do so. One might say that one of the attractions of his philosophy derives in good part from the fact that he carries far each of two great tendencies of the human spirit: the realistic tendency to insist upon

things as almost impervious to the mind; the ideal-
istic tendency, so recurrent in German philosophy,
to locate everything in the mind. Thus, Heidegger
will say on the one hand that truth consists in "let-
ting things go," that truth is in things, and is a prop-
erty of things, not of judgments; on the other hand,
that the source of truth lies in our freedom. And at
times it seems that this freedom, in turn, should be
defined as the capacity to surrender to things. In
the latter case, the realistic element triumphs. But
the problem remains, essentially unresolved.

We can see that the philosophy of Heidegger contains a certain number of heterogeneous elements.
The notion of the experience of anguish, and marked
Kierkegaardian influences, lead to a definition of
human existence as anxious, bent over itself, making
plans. On the other hand, the Heideggerian individual is in-the-world, an idea which is foreign to
Kierkegaard and may have come in part from Husserl. And we must not forget the metaphysic or
ontology, and the importance assigned to the notion of Being. It is the fusion of Kierkegaardian
elements, affirmations of being-in-the-world, and
ontology which gives to the philosophy of Heidegger its particular tonality.

Before embarking on a critical exploration of the
philosophy of Heidegger, we may notice that the
first two elements in this fusion are linked. Existence

is anxious, not only because it is drawn towards the future, but because it is in the world; and "the being-in-the-world" assumes the form of forlornness because experience is pervaded and gripped by anxiety. We sense in this philosophy both a tendency towards an extreme individuality and a tendency towards a deeply-felt totality.

*

*    *

This sketch of the philosophy of Heidegger leads to some further considerations. Taken as a whole, does not this doctrine imply a *Weltanschauung* which is negated by the doctrine itself? There is no place for God, it seems, in the philosophy of Heidegger; and yet, when he depicts us as forlorn, and even guilty, is there not—at least, in these expressions—an echo of the religious ideas among which he grew up and the religious influences which accompanied the early developments of his thought and philosophy? We might venture to say that some of the essential notions in his philosophy arise from a certain level of thought which he believed he had passed beyond. Could it be that if Heidegger were completely free of his religious presuppositions, he would cease to be Heidegger? Midway between Kierkegaard and Nietzsche, he is in the world of Nietzsche with the

feelings of Kierkegaard and in the world of Kierkegaard with the feelings of Nietzsche.

In the second place, could we not conceive of a
philosophy of existence linked, not solely to experiences of separation, forlornness, and profound mel-
ancholy, but also to feelings of hope and confidence?
This objection to Heidegger has often been voiced
by Gabriel Marcel. The Heideggerian doubtless
would reply that, existence being finite and ourselves being destined for death, there is no cause
for such hope and confidence. But does the thought
of death reveal more of the existence and condition
of Man than the thought of life? Certain passages in
Sartre's *L'Être et le Néant (Being and Nothingness)*
challenge Heidegger on this very point and tend to
minimize the idea of death which is of first importance in the philosophy of Heidegger.

In the third place, we may question whether certain ideas have been adequately defined; in particular, the ideas of Being and Possibility. The idea of
Possibility, though used by Kierkegaard, Jaspers,
and Heidegger, is nowhere made precise, except
perhaps in the work of Sartre. And the attempt to
throw some light—a dim enough light, as it happens
—upon the idea of Nothingness is, in the last
analysis, more intriguing than satisfying.

Lastly, our assessment brings us to Heidegger's
moral conclusions. The "resolute decision," by which

we take upon ourselves our destiny, constitutes a sort of act of faith, understandable in Nietzsche as a pure act of the creative will of values, but less clearly substantiated in Heidegger. Moreover, this "resolute decision" remains extremely formal. How does one proceed from theory to practice? Heidegger himself has applied it differently at different times, doubtless according to the lessons he believed to be furnished by experience; but we cannot set aside the fact that at the time of the formation and initial triumphs of Nazism, his "resolute decision" was to follow the lead of the Nazi chiefs. This may not have been—contrary to his belief at the time and to the belief of his adversaries to this day—an absolutely logical consequence of his philosophy. But we may conclude from this evidence that the ethics of Heidegger remains purely formal, admits of several interpretations, and finally, is not an ethics at all.

❁

❁          ❁

We come now to the third stage in this brief history of the philosophy of existence.

Several young and able French philosophers have found in the ideas of Heidegger something fresh and significant which answers to their own feeling of anguish. There was already in France—particularly in the philosophy of Gabriel Marcel—something which could be compared to the philosophy of Jaspers and Heidegger. Furthermore, the influence of Heidegger was directly felt in France before the war—though, to be sure, in a small circle of thinkers.

The philosophy of Sartre, although containing much that is original with him, is linked in part to the philosophy of Heidegger and in part to that of Husserl. The latter leads him into a kind of idealism which may not be completely consonant with the elements which he may have derived from Heidegger. In common with Heidegger, Sartre has "the ontological concern," the need to study the idea of Being, and also an emphasis on the idea of Nothingness, though for Sartre this latter idea is often rendered in a sense more Hegelian than Heideggerian. Sartre characterizes Being as having two forms: "in-itself" (*l'en-soi*), which is always identical with itself and corresponds to what is extended for Descartes; and "for-itself" (*le pour-soi*), which corresponds to Thought construed in Hegelian fashion as a constant movement.

Which is primary, the "in-itself" or the "for-itself"? This is one of the most difficult of all problems to resolve in the philosophy of Sartre. When he says that the "in-itself" is primary, he classifies himself as a realist; when he emphasizes the "for-itself," he classifies himself as an idealist. The "for-itself" appears to be a Nothingness, or more precisely, a nullification; following a comparison drawn by Gabriel Marcel, we might say that the "for-itself" is a kind of *trou d'air* or vent in the "in-itself." This conception is not dissimilar to Bergson's conception of consciousness as being primarily selection.

Inasmuch as these two forms of being are absolutely opposed to each other in all their characteristics, one is tempted to ask if it is proper to call both of them Being. If ontology is the science of a unique being, can there be any ontology in this ontological theory?

In the second place, one may question if there actually is something in reality which can be the "in-itself" as defined by Sartre; that is to say, something purely and uniquely itself. On this point the Hegelian theory, in which the Absolute is the development of the implicit "for-itself" towards an explicit "for-itself" seems far more satisfactory. No doubt, Sartre's affirmation of the "in-itself" responds to an epistemological concern on his part, and answered the need to affirm a reality independent of thought; but has one the right to pass from this assertion to the notion that this reality is what it is, and is uniquely so—is, in fact, something massive and stable?

On a good many points, as we have said, Sartre

is an idealist. But by his insistence upon the intentionality of consciousness, by his definition of knowledge as a "not-being," by his conception of a massive "in-itself" to which consciousness opposes itself as a Nothingness, by his affirmation of radical contingency, and by his insistence on the failure inherent in love-relationships, he seems to summarize the frequently justifiable grounds for the modern world's animadversions to idealism.

Perhaps the duality of Sartre's philosophy is one of its intrinsic characteristics, and not to be disprized. A search for justification and the impossibility of justification are recurrent *motifs* in the philosophy of Sartre. His philosophy is one of the incarnations of problematism and of the ambiguity of contemporary thought (for Man does seem, to the contemporary mind, to be ambiguous).

This is not to say that an effort by Sartre to dispel ambiguity is either inadvisable or improbable. There is the Sartre of *Nausea* and the Sartre of *The Flies*. There is the Sartre of *Morts Sans Sépultures*, which reflects divergent and contrary aspects of Sartre. There may yet be a Sartre who will go beyond ambiguity.

*
*　　　*

A few summary remarks are suggested by this brief survey of the philosophers of existence. Kierkegaard is not at all interested in ontology, and in this respect he is more existential than Heidegger or Sartre. Thus, in the history of the philosophy of existence, one goes from a consideration of existence proper to a study of Being with the help of the idea of existence. The latter method is that of Heidegger and Sartre. Nevertheless, Sartre and Heidegger differ considerably, and Sartre is closer than Heidegger to Kierkegaard. For example, Sartre criticizes the pre-eminence which Heidegger assigns to the ontological over the ontic.

We might mention, without discussing, Simone de Beauvoir and Merleau-Ponty, whose theories are similar to those of Sartre, though sometimes applied in different domains of experience. We must omit discussion of those who, like Bataille and Camus, are often classed as existentialists, but who would refuse to accept the appellation.

Let us construct a few rules-of-thumb for distinguishing between existentialists and non-existentialists. If we say: "Man is in this world, a world limited by death and experienced in anguish; is aware of himself as essentially anxious; is burdened by his solitude within the horizon of his temporality"; then we recognize the accents of Heideggerian philosophy. If we say: "Man, by opposition to the 'in-itself' is the 'for-itself,' is never at rest, and strives in vain towards a union of the 'in-itself' and the 'for-itself' "; then we are speaking in the manner of Sartrian existentialism. If we say: "I am a thinking thing," as Descartes said; or, "The real things are Ideas," as Plato said; or, "The Ego accompanies all our representations," as Kant said; then we are moving in a sphere which is no longer that of the philosophy of existence.

⚬

⚬    ⚬

The philosophy of existence reminds us, once more, of what all great philosophy has tried to teach us: that there are views of reality which cannot be completely reduced to scientific formulations. Naturally, those who are of the contrary opinion will still try to explain the philosophy of existence scientifically; for example, by economic or historical reasons. Such explanations often have some validity, but they are never completely satisfactory.

Thanks to existentialism, to be or not to be has again become the question. And this reminds us that there have been many existentialists—or, as Kierkegaard would say, many existents. We have just intimated that Hamlet was an existent. We could say the same of Pascal; of Lequier, the philosopher from whom Sartre has borrowed the dictum: *"Faire, et en faisant, se faire*"; of Carlyle; and of William James. We could say the same of Socrates' great enemy, Nietzsche. We could show that the origins of most great philosophies, like those of Plato, Descartes, and Kant, are to be found in existential reflections.

There is, however, a question which may trouble the mind, and even the existence, of the existentialist. Does he not risk destroying the very existence which he wishes above all to preserve? Jaspers rejected the term "existentialist." Kierkegaard did not wish to construct a philosophy; one may go even further, for not only would Kierkegaard have refused the name "existentialist," not only would he have rejected the term "philosopher of existence," but doubtless in his Christian humility he would have refused the name "existent." Is it for the existent to say that he exists? In short, is it, perhaps, necessary to choose between existentialism and existence? Such is the dilemma of existentialism.

At any rate, it is clear that one of the consequences of the existentialist movement and the philosophies of existence is that we have to destroy the majority of the ideas of so-called "philosophical common-sense," and of what has often been called "the eternal philosophy." In particular, we have to destroy the ideas of Essence and Substance. Philosophy—so goes the new affirmation—must cease to be philosophy of essence and must become philosophy of existence. We are observing a whole philosophical movement which dislodges previous philosophical concepts, and which tends to make more acute our subjective understanding at the same time as it makes us feel more strongly than ever our union with the world. In this sense, we are witnessing and participating in the beginning of a new mode of philosophizing.

We see that the negations advanced by the philosophers of existence imply some affirmations; in Heidegger, for example, the affirmation of our unity with the world. Doubtless we have also noticed, in reviewing rapidly the various philosophies of existence, that we find ourselves time and again before impasses. In Heidegger, for example, we do not know if his system is an idealism or a realism; if the Nothingness is Nothingness or Being. There is a similar impasse in Sartre, and on certain points a return, perhaps even a recoil, from the conceptions of Heidegger towards those of Hegel and Husserl. But these impasses need not turn us back. The permanence of the dogmatisms under whose banners the philosophy of existence is attacked are themselves reasons for reaffirming the importance and the leading role of the philosophy of existence. All great philosophies have encountered such impasses, but thought has gone ahead and somehow found a solution. Perhaps, in order to facilitate an egress from these difficulties, it will be necessary to distinguish more and more carefully among the different elements which we have enumerated, e.g., the insistence upon existence, and the insistence upon being-in-the-world. No doubt there are different levels and elements in reality; but it is only by distinguishing the various problems, levels, and elements in these philosophies of existence, and assessing their relative importance, that we will be able to gain an insight into their difficulties and possibly pass beyond them.

## DISCUSSION

NICOLAS BERDIAEFF:

In my opinion, your description of the philosophy of Heidegger was astoundingly clear; for it is not an easy subject. However, although you have made some important points, I am not entirely satisfied with the way in which you have treated the question of the relationship between Kierkegaard and Heidegger. I find that the difference between Heidegger and Kierkegaard is colossal, and that perhaps even the influence of Kierkegaard is exaggerated. Kierkegaard's philosophy of existence is an expressionistic philosophy—one might say: is the expression of the existence of Kierkegaard; here, the knowing subject is existential. He did not wish to create an ontology or a metaphysics, and he did not believe in the possibility of an ideational philosophy; he believed only in an expression of existence. I think that Jaspers is much closer to Kierkegaard. And yet, both he and Sartre differ widely from Kierkegaard, because both wanted to create an ontology; which is, in my opinion, an absolute contradiction. Ontology is impossible from the existential point of view. Jaspers was certainly nearer the truth when he said that the only possibility would be a perusal of ciphers, a symbolic knowledge far removed from any rational ontology. Yet Heidegger and Sartre want to create a rational ontology, Sartre even more than Heidegger.

Moreover, I am not at all sure that the idea of Nothingness in Sartre approximates the idea of Nothingness in Hegel. For Hegel, Nothingness has positive results, because the future comes from, and exists only by virtue of, this Nothingness. I do not see this in Sartre. Rather, I have the impression that according to Sartre being begins to decompose or rot internally under the influence of Nothingness. Nothingness is putrefaction of being. This is not at all Hegel's notion, and he would never have said such a thing.

Why is an ontology impossible? Because it is always a knowledge objectifying existence. In an ontology the idea of Being is objectified, and an objectification is already an existence which is alienated in the objectification. So that in ontology—in every ontology—existence vanishes. There is no more existence because existence cannot be objectified. It is precisely in this respect that I feel myself rather close to Kierkegaard, although in other respects I am not at all partial to him. It is only in subjectivity that one may know existence, not in objectivity. In my opinion, the central idea has vanished in the ontology of Heidegger and Sartre.

Jaspers remains closer to existence because he did not hold to this. I have much more sympathy for the philosophy of Jaspers, though you assign much more importance to that of Heidegger. I believe that Jaspers is more nearly right than Heidegger. He is much nearer to Kierkegaard and Nietzsche.

One might also ask the question: is the philosophy of Nietzsche an existential philosophy? But, at any rate, he is an existential philosopher in the same sense as Kierkegaard, quite in the same sense. I could not say the same of Heidegger or Sartre. I think this is the central problem.

GEORGES GURVITCH:

First of all, I would like to congratulate Jean Wahl on having been able to say *No* to the student who asked him if he was an existentialist. I would even like to hope that this *No* will eventually grow into complete non-acceptance.*

The term "existence" introduced by Kierkegaard, and the philosophy of existence of which he was the promoter, had a definite historical significance as weapons against the constructive dialectic and pan-logism of Hegel. Moreover, there is no doubt about the fact that "existence" for Kierkegaard was primarily that of Christ—transcendence incarnated in immanence, Jesus initiating a lineage of "existents" who teach by the very fact of existing. Like most doctrines, the philosophy of existence is right in what it denies and wrong in what it affirms.

In Heidegger—who is not an honest thinker, but an able constructor and calculator bereft of ethics and intellectual scruples—the philosophy of exist-ence has lost its negative sincerity: it has become a mere means dexterously used to pass from the scho-lastic philosophy in which he began to the Nazi philosophy.

Sartre's *L'Être et le Néant* proclaims a possible liaison between the logomachy of Hegel and the philosophy of existence. To become "existentialism," existence first passes through the logonomical purga-tory of "in-itself" and "for-itself" to rediscover itself —impoverished to the limit. If one could accept the

---

* In the original, this paragraph contains a play on words which is untranslatable.—Tr.

opening chapters of the work of Sartre, I believe one could just as easily, and far more sensibly, accept purely and simply: Hegel or dialectical materialism, neither of which is bereft, as is existentialism, of consequences and a sense of history.

And if one attaches some importance to the notion of existence, at least as a battle against "essences" and all the traditional and acquired philosophic positions, one must note that in no philosophy is existence found to be more impoverished or diluted than precisely in: "existentialism." In Kierkegaard it had already been artificially reduced to the Religious and the Individual. In Sartre it becomes a psychological isolation which nullifies itself, and only tangentially does he arrive at "the other." One affirms existence after one has carefully emptied it of all its richness, all its contradictions, all its collective and historical aspects! The call to existence becomes an evasion, a replacement·of constructed existence for lived existence.

History repeats itself. As the traditional empiricism amounted to a total destruction or transformation of experience into a chaos of sensation, so existentialism applies itself to the task of reducing existence to zero. This is the nausea of impotence.

JEAN WAHL:

I could not let pass, without registering a protest,

the remarks of my friend Gurvitch, whose concluding words were perhaps more forceful than pre-
meditated.

ALEXANDRE KOYRÉ: *

To begin with, I was a little surprised that in his
brilliant exposition, M. Wahl spoke so little of a
concept—essential, so I believe—to Heidegger: the
concept of Anxiety. Existence, according to Heidegger, is subjected to Anxiety; not the multiple anxi-
eties of daily life, but to Anxiety as such. Existence
is dominated in its entirety by the fact of Anxiety.
This, for the very simple reason that existence is
essentially finite. Heidegger says somewhere that
the finitude of being is closer to us than we ourselves
are. This finitude, in simple terms, means death.
That is what determines existence, the mode of
existence of man. When Heidegger speaks of
*Dasein*,* it is of Man that he is speaking, and he says
so himself in his little tract on truth. There is the
essential fact.

The human being exists as a mortal and is the
only being who knows—who can know—that he is
mortal. It is this inexorable limit—mortality, finitude,
death—which determines and characterizes him,

* Acknowledgment is due to Mr. Moré for permission to reproduce
the text of the remarks of Messrs. Koyré, Gandillac, and Marcel, as it
appeared in the review *Dieu Vivant*, number 6.
* "Being-there" or "being-in-the-world."—Tr.

plus the fact that he knows it, that he is the only being in the world who knows it. As we are in reality; as we are in essence; *so* must we be. Which is to say, we must be clairvoyant and reveal what we truly are, without dissimulating to ourselves by all the artifices and masks of the distraction of life itself.

It is this awareness of our mortality, of death, that constitutes decision and acceptance. Heidegger echoes the ancient theme of wisdom: wisdom is always the acceptance of what is. If we have done that—if the existent being has done that—then we arrive at that authenticity which reveals ourself to ourself and, at the same time, permits us to reveal what we are. And there you see the function of authenticity: if I am truly authentic, then I am true, then I can reveal Being as it is. If I am unaware of all this, I fall into the inauthentic. I disguise my reality and my essence from myself, and thereby become incapable of perceiving and revealing reality as it really is.

To say to Heidegger: "One must not think of death, one must think of life; as Spinoza said, of hope; the future is hope!" is all very well. But the spinozistic 'life,' the spinozistic or kantian 'hope,' rest upon a metaphysics or a theology. Heidegger wants neither metaphysics nor theology; and in his recent pamphlet on the essence of truth, he says very succinctly (in a little note that contains what is perhaps most important in the tract) that we are going towards a supercession (*Ueberwindung*) of metaphysics. His man is a man without metaphysics and without religion, a man who finds himself flung into the world. I do not think that the translation "forlornness" (*délaissement*) expresses his thought very well; we are thrown into the world. We are there; I am there such as I am; and I neither know why nor how; the only thing I know, truly and inexorably, is that some day I am going to die. And that is what limits all my possibilities and my future. My future limited, finite, and I knowing it—*that* is my situation in the world. I know that my existence is precarious and short, and that I can lose it. This is the only thing that I have, and I can lose it at any moment; that is why there is the substratum of anxiety, fear, and anguish. I do not see the difficulties that have been found in this doctrine.

MAURICE DE GANDILLAC:

There may still be a grave obscurity. You said: It's very simple . . . You even used the word "essence" at that time, in a manner which perhaps was not entirely wished-for. In other words, that which we discover is something like a "nature" or an "essence." An essence of which we know nothing, since there is no previous metaphysics or theology. Nevertheless, we discover without a doubt that we are going to die. But is this simply a fact or a sort of right? Can one say that it is our nature to be beings made for death? Can one say that the essence of man is to be finite? In that case, it seems to me that one would go singularly beyond the point of departure, even from the philosophical point of view, of what is existential, which is precisely to know that existence is anterior to any determination of nature.

ALEXANDRE KOYRÉ:

In my opinion, that is mostly a terminological dispute; the terms "nature" and "essence" are vague enough; if you define "nature" as it used to be defined in scholastic philosophy, then you have a being determined in all its operations, and all its actions flow from its determinations. It is clear that, in this sense, the Heideggerian *Dasein* is neither a "nature" nor an "essence." It is true, nevertheless, that *Dasein* does possess an essential structure. One might say, for example, that our existence is essentially finite, without thereby going beyond Heideggerian thought. There *is* the finitude which is absolutely essential; and that is the foundation of his thought. Existence is always mine, and has to do with myself. And it is always finite for each of us. There is an essential finitude; and in that sense I would use the term "essence" without discomfiture. Finitude is something essential to the human being, and I might even say that it forms its essence.

MAURICE DE GANDILLAC:

My objection certainly went beyond the question of vocabulary, and here is exactly what I mean: Can one think the notion of the tragedy of this finitude in itself, if one does not first posit an infinitude or a right to the infinite, a right to immortality? Is it not in an essentially religious perspective, which first posits immortality, that mortality, finitude, takes on its character . . . ? And does the consciousness of being "for death" constitute a necessarily privileged structure confined to the experience of Heidegger?

ALEXANDRE KOYRÉ:

That is a very difficult question and one may answer it in a number of different ways. One may maintain (as has been held, and as I am inclined to believe) that the finite implies the infinite. One cannot define finitude except by negation. But you know that is an opinion not shared by everyone. It is a Cartesian argument.

You say that the fear of death *implies* the desire for, or the right to, the immortality which we feel deprived of. I don't know. It may be, on the contrary, the fear of death which *founded* the desire for immortality, the hope for immortality, the notion of projecting man into immortality, and the hope of prolonging a life whose finitude is known. Evidently that is the viewpoint of Heidegger. I believe that it is perfectly tenable, that one does not need to believe oneself immortal to be afraid of death, and that finitude, the fact of disappearance and end, despite all the epicurean considerations, remains an agonizing fact. This is what Heidegger tries to unveil, or make us aware of, in his analysis of anguish. Through anguish, it seems to him, we discover the foundation of Nothingness on which we are perched, or from which we are come—an ocean of Nothingness, from which we painfully emerge for a time, but which is always there to swallow us, and in which we are always about to sink.

GABRIEL MARCEL:

I wanted to say a-word during the preceding discussion, in regard to what M. Koyré said. I am convinced that Sartre is right on this point. Moreover, I am always very struck by the profound ambiguity of Heideggerian terminology. *"Zum Tode sein"* can not be translated into French. You have said: *"être vers la mort"* (to be towards death), which was a correct translation—but what does it mean? Does *"zum Tode sein"* really mean "to be destined for death," or does it perhaps mean "to be delivered up to death"? Therein lies a far-reaching equivocation, and consequently I am not at all in agreement with M. Koyré. There is nothing in all this, to my mind, that is self-evident.

Furthermore, one does not know just what to believe about this kind of thing which, in this case, is in no way an induction, but which reveals to us that we are mortal beings. I wonder if one does not really have to deal with history, and, as our poor friend Landsberg said, put the accent on war, on the fact of the imminence of death in war; which would enormously reduce the universal import of the experience, but would accentuate the existential character of Heideggerian thought. But that would absolutely not permit us to construct, as M. Koyré seemed to be suggesting, an "authentic" truth—because, if it is truth at all, it is truth at the "inauthentic" level, the level of *Man* or "Everyman."

And now I come to a final question. To recapitulate what M. Koyré said: he who takes refuge in a metaphysics or a religion, lives in the inauthentic sphere. But I ask: can this being, who takes refuge in a metaphysics, be assimilated into this *Man* or "everyman" which is the subject of the inauthentic experience? It seems to me that these are two different matters, and if Heidegger means to make them equivalent, he is guilty of a great confusion. What he attacks is a certain contemptible commonplaceness, a certain dastardliness, if you like, about a common existence which, in effect, consists of dissimulating the imminence of death and taking refuge in pastimes. But may we really, in the name of any sound anthropology, identify that with the experience of the wise Hindu? That is an absurdity. So that, in reality, all this experience of *zum Tode sein* which has the air of being central and cogent seems to me extraordinarily fragile; and (to repeat) I, who can not be suspected of an excessive sympathy for the thought of Sartre on this matter, find his analysis more honest and more sound.

EMMANUEL LEVINAS:

I would like to go back to two questions raised by M. Wahl. The first concerns the definition of existentialism. The second is relative to the reflection concerning the notion of death: why should the thought of death be more revealing than the thought of life? This question carries a criticism of Heidegger which we often hear, in different forms—a criticism which I do not wish to refute for the sake of following Heidegger, but which I would like to consider in order to explain Heidegger.

You have even raised a third question: who is existentialist? And you were able to find existentialists everywhere. There is existentialism farther back than Kierkegaard and Pascal, in Shakespeare and Socrates; and nowhere: because everyone disavows it. This is what Husserl called the second stage in the spread of a new doctrine. During the first stage, one cries: it's absurd! During the second stage, one says indignantly: but everybody knows that! There is a third stage, in which the doctrine is reinstated in its true originality.

This multiplication of a modern doctrine down through the past fortunately will end in its own negation. Then, perhaps, we will come to realize that there is only one existentialist or philosopher of existence, and that this one and only existentialist is neither Kierkegaard, nor Nietzsche, nor Socrates, nor even—despite all the talent deployed—some one of the successors of Heidegger. The only existentialist is Heidegger himself, who rejects the term.

Why Heidegger? Because the metaphysical accomplishments of Heidegger have furnished the light by which we are able to discern existentialism in the night of the past where, it seems, it was hidden. This is even true in respect to Kierkegaard. It is possible that behind each phrase of Heidegger there is some Kierkegaardian thought—certainly, Kierkegaard was well known in Germany and even in France, as Henri Delacroix and Victor Basch had written on him at the beginning of this century—but it is thanks to Heidegger that this train of thought has sounded a philosophical note. I mean that, prior to Heidegger, Kierkegaard was confined to the provinces of essay, psychology, aesthetics, or theology, and that after Heidegger, he came into the purview of philosophy.

In what did it consist—this transformation, which was the achievement of Heidegger?

It consisted in retrieving those thoughts which may be called "pathetic," disseminated over the length and breadth of history, and restoring them to those landmarks, those points of reference, which —despite all the discredit that their official status assigns them—are endowed with an exceptional degree of intelligibility: namely, the categories of the professors of philosophy—Plato, Aristotle, Kant, Hegel, etc. Heidegger restored pathetic thoughts to the categories of the professors.

To enter into Heideggerian thought, it is not enough to show its systematic coherence, and the manner in which are linked the notions which begin to trail through the streets and *cafés*—Anguish, Death, Dereliction, the Ecstasies of Times, etc. In re-ascending towards the categories—towards the ever-renewed light which emanates from these intellectual myths—one must ask: In what does the essential category of Heideggerian existentialism consist which casts its particular illumination on all those notions whereby the existentialists describe man, and transforms the old notions into new philosophy.

Well, I think that the new philosophical "twist" originated by Heidegger consists in distinguishing between *Being* and *being* (thing or person), and in giving to *Being* the relation, the movement, the efficacy which until then resided in the existent. Existentialism is to experience and think existence—the verb "to be"—as event, an event which neither produces that which exists, nor is the action of what exists upon another object. It is the pure fact of existing which is event. The fact of existing, until then pure and reticent and tranquil; the fact which, in the Aristotelian notion of the act, remained quite serene and equal to itself among all the adventures that befall a being; the fact which was transcendent to all *being*, but which was not itself the event of transcending; this fact appears in existentialism as the adventure itself, containing History in itself.

When Heidegger says "being-in-the-world" and "being-for-death" and "being-with-others," what he adds that is new to our millenary knowledge of our mortality, our social nature, and our presence in the world, is that these prepositions—"in," "for," and "with" are in the root of the verb "to be" (as "ex" is in the root of the verb "to exist"); that these phrases are not created by us as existents placed in determinate conditions; that they are not even mathematically contained, as in Husserl, in our nature or our essence as existents; that they are neither contingent nor necessary attributes of our substance; and finally, that they *are* articulations of the event of *being*, heretofore considered to be tranquil, simple, equal to itself. One may say that existentialism consists in feeling and thinking that the verb "to be" is transitive.

When in his novels (I have not yet read *L'Être et le Néant*) Sartre italicizes the verb "to be," and underlines "am" in "I *am* that suffering" or "I *am* that nothingness," it is this transitiveness of the verb "to be" that he is trying to accentuate.

Thus, in existential philosophy there are no longer any copulas. The copulas express the very event of being.

I think that a certain use of the verb "to be"—which does not mean that I give to Being a purely verbal signification—corresponding to this notion of transitiveness, is more characteristic of this philosophy than the evocation of ecstasies, anxiety, or death, which are in themselves as nietzschean or christian as they are existentialist.

But do not the categories of "potentiality" and "act" suffice to express this new notion of existence? Is not existence which passes into act at the stage where it is merely potentiality for that event of transition?

I do not think so—and here I have an opportunity to reply to the second question raised by M. Jean

Wahl: why did Heidegger choose Death rather than, for example, Hope, to characterize existence?

A potentiality which passes into act: this describes an existent which least resembles a tranquil existence, self-contained and situated outside of existence and events. By this very fact, its existence is its realization, a constant loss of what makes it a simple possibility. The realization of power is an event of neutralization.

In order that power may inevitably constitute *being*, in order that *being* may inevitably be event, it is necessary that power be defined otherwise than by reference to the act, and that it be outside of finality. The event of existence must be other than the realization of a pre-existing goal. So, Heidegger says: death is such an event. To realize the possibility of death is to realize the impossibility of all realization—to be in the possible-as-such and not in a possible "image of immobile eternity." One may also say that Heidegger replaces "finality" by "a relation with an end" (in the ordinary sense of the term "end," and not in the sense of "goal").

Heidegger needs a possibility which is neither the consequence nor the precursor of the act; then he detaches the notion of possibility from the notion of the act. Which permits possibility ever to remain possibility, so much so that the moment at which it is exhausted is: death. The notion of death allows possibility to be thought and seized as possibility: it is part of this fundamental intuition; it is the event of existence I do not know if you agree with me.

Existence produces itself in such a manner that each being is already hurling himself towards death, and this manner of hurling himself towards death is, for him, a possibility *par excellence*, because all other possibilities fulfill themselves and become acts, whereas death becomes non-reality, non-being. That is the sense in which Heidegger says that death is the possibility of impossibility.

JEAN WAHL:

In my opinion, Kierkegaard sheds, in his *Concluding Unscientific Postscript*, all possible light on this notion of existence which, like Schelling and more so than Schelling, he placed at the center of his thought. It is not through Heidegger that one discovers Kierkegaard, even if, sociologically and historically speaking, many have done so (some people would not have cared to read Hegel if Marx had not existed). It is not from Heidegger that the historians of thought like Delacroix and Basch (and a good many Germans) found out about Kierkegaard. Moreover, many discovered him not through Heidegger but through Barth, whom Levinas has not mentioned. But no matter. . . . It is not thanks to Heidegger that the phrases of Kierkegaard sounded a philosophic note, unless we understand by this phrase: relative to the philosophy of the school, relative to the philosophy of professors. There is a complete divergence between us on the meaning of the word "philosophy," which I continue not to reserve for the class of professors or the professors of classes.

Furthermore: nothing more severe for Heidegger than the words of Levinas. Heidegger would restore pathetic thoughts to the categories of professors . . .! This is to accuse him both as a Benda would, and as I unhesitatingly would (despite all my admiration of him).

Let us also note that Kant, and before him Gaunilon perhaps, and many others before Heidegger (I have already mentioned Schelling) saw existence as event, as fact; saw it with great clarity and expressed it with great mastery, all the while circumventing ontology.

To be sure, there is in Heidegger, as Levinas indicates, the profundity of what I would call an intuition of the feeling of being; but it is hidden by the ontological language. Levinas tries to show that existentialism and ontology can go together (but let us not forget that Heidegger rejects the term "existentialism"). He could not succeed because ontology traffics in words. And let us add that if what he says is true; if the word "to be" supports the flexions "with," "in-the-world," and "for-death" in its very essence (here, again, I note a paradox), then we have not an ontology, but rather, ontologies.

As to the role of Death, I am in accord with Levinas (and Aristotle) and the critics of Aristotle, in saying that a power which passes into the act implies the act (moreover, this is a tautology). A possibility, in realizing itself, "de-possibilizes" itself. But far from being an impossibility of realization, death is the realization itself, that is to say, the "thingification." Thus, it is not true that to realize the possibility of death is to realize the possible as such. Moreover, if death is, as Levinas says in commenting on Heidegger, the end of all possibility, it cannot be the root of the possible.

*

* *

NICOLAS BERDIAEFF, the late Russian philosopher and author, many of whose books have been translated into English; "personalist" philosopher who often verged on mysticism.

MAURICE DE GANDILLAC, professor in the Sorbonne, Paris, and author of works on medieval and Renaissance philosophy.

GEORGES GURVITCH, sociologist and theoretician of law who has written on Fichte, Proudhon, and various social problems; professor at the Sorbonne.

ALEXANDRE KOYRÉ, professor in Ecole des Hautes-Etudes, Sorbonne, and currently lecturing at the University of Chicago; best known for his writings on Plato, Jacob, Boehme, Descartes, and Galileo.

EMMANUEL LEVINAS, former student of Heidegger, now creating an original philosophy; author of *De l'Existence à l'Existant*.

GABRIEL MARCEL, the most representative philosopher of Christian existentialism in France.

# INDEX

Aristotle, 50, 55
"authentic sphere of existence," 11, 12, 46

Barth, Karl, 53
Basch, Victor, 48, 53
Bataille, 31
*Being and Nothingness (L'Être et le Néant)*, 26, 38
*Being and Time (Sein und Zeit)*, 22, 23, 51
Benda, 54
Berdiaeff, Nicolas, discussion by, 35–37
Bergson, Henri, 29

Camus, Albert, 31
Carlyle, Thomas, 33
Communication, 11
*Concluding Unscientific Postscript*, 53

*Dasein*, 40, note 40, 43
*das Man*, note 12, 46
*das Verständnis*, 17
de Beauvoir, Simone, 2, 31
de Gandillac, Maurice, discussion by, 42–43, 44
Descartes, René, 3, 15, 28, 32, 33, 44

"ecstasies of time," 18, 48
"ecstasy of existence," 15
empiricism, 39
"everyman," 12, 19, 46
existentialism, application of term, 2; and communication, 11; and Hegel, 3; and Plato, 2; problem of defining, 1–2; and Spinoza, 2; summary remarks on, 31–32; vagueness of term, 1
Existentials, 21

Farber, Marvin, 1
Fichte, Johann G., 23
"for-itself," the, 28, 29, 30

Gaunilon, 54
God, 5, 6, 7, 14, 15, 25
Gurvitch, Georges, discussion by, 37–39

Hamlet, 32
Hegel, Georg W. F., 2, 6, 7, 8, 9, 13, 14, 19, 28, 29, 34, 36, 38, 39, 53; and Kierkegaard, 3, 6, 8; rationality of, 3
Heidegger, Martin, Anxiety, 14, 40, 42, 49; *Being and Time Sein und Zeit*), 22, 23, 51; *Dasein*, 40, note 40, 43; *das Man*, 12, note 12, 19, 46; death, 14, 40, 41, 43, 44, 45–47, 48, 52–53, 55; ethics of, 21–22, 26–27; God, 15, 25; idealism vs. realism, 23–24, 34; Leibniz, 16; Nothingness, 12–13, 17, 26, 34, 35; philosophy, definition of, 20; time, 18, 19, 22, 48; transcendence, 15–17; truth, 24, 42
Hölderlin, 23
Husserl, Edmund, 24, 28, 34, 48, 50

# INDEX

Ibsen, Henrik, 5
"in-itself," the, 28, 29, 30, 38
"inauthentic sphere of existence,"
  2, 11, 12, 46

James, William, 33
Jaspers, Karl, 1, 12, 17, 27, 28,
  33, 36; and Kierkegaard, 9–11
Jesus, 9, 10, 38

Kant, Immanuel, 8, 16, 32, 33,
  54
Kierkegaard, Sören, and Christianity, 5; on choice, 4–5; on
  the existent, 4, 6; on God, 5,
  6, 7; opposition to Hegel, 3, 6;
  philosophy of, 3–9; subjectivity
  of, 3–5
Koyré, Alexandre, discussion by,
  40–42, 42–43, 44–45

"l'en-soi," 28, 29, 38
L'Être et le Néant (Being and
  Nothingness), 26, 38, 51
Leibniz, 16
"le pour-soi," 28, 29, 30, 38
Lequier, 32
Levinas, Emmanuel, 22, 53, 54,
  55; discussion by, 47–53

Marcel, Gabriel, 26, 28, 29; discussion by, 45–47
Marx, Karl, 53

Merleau-Ponty, 2, 31
Morts Sans Sépultures, 30

Nausea, 30
Nazism, and Heidegger, 27
"Nichten," 13
Nietzsche, Friedrich, 10, 15, 19,
  22, 27, 33, 37, 48

ontology, 11, 36–37, 54, 55

Parmenides, 18
Pascal, Blaise, 8, 32, 47
Plato, 2, 14, 32, 33

"resolute decision," 19, 22, 26–27
Rilke, Rainer, 23

Saint Augustine, 8
Sartre, Jean-Paul, 1, 2, 11, 22,
  26, 31, 34, 36, 37, 38, 39, 45,
  47, 51; philosophy of, 27–30
Schelling, 8, 54
Sein und Zeit (Being and Time),
  22, 23, 51
Shakespeare, 47
Socrates, 33, 47, 48
Spinoza, 2

The Flies, 30
transcendence, according to Heidegger, 15–17